PABLO
PICASSO

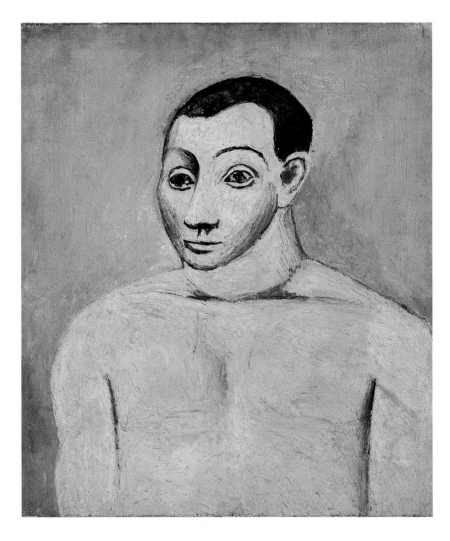

PABLO
PICASSO

JESSE McDONALD

BARNES
&NOBLE
BOOKS
NEW YORK

This edition published by
Barnes and Noble Inc..
by arrangement with Brompton
Books Corporation

Produced by Brompton Books
Corporation
15 Sherwood Place
Greenwich. CT 06830

ISBN 1-56619-182-3

Printed in Hong Kong

PAGE 1: *Self-Portrait*, 1906. oil on
canvas, Picasso Museum, Paris

PAGE 2: *Three Women*, 1907-8. oil
on canvas, Museum of Modern Art,
Moscow

PAGE 4: *Man with Mandolin*, 1911.
oil on canvas, Picasso Museum, Paris

CONTENTS

INTRODUCTION

The genius of Pablo Picasso, most famous, versatile and prolific artist of the twentieth century, has provoked countless critics and art historians to try to account for his extraordinary vitality and creativity in the context of his richly unconventional life. Although renowned above all for his painting, he was also a skilled and original sculptor, graphic artist, ceramicist and designer, whose influence on twentieth century art is incalculable. He is associated primarily with the development of Cubism from 1907 onward, which finally abandoned the European Renaissance tradition that art should imitate life. The Impressionists and their successors had already undermined this dogma, but it was Picasso who achieved the final breakthrough. At first even the most avant-garde of his contemporaries were shocked and baffled by the early Cubist works. Henri Matisse and André Derain both reacted with horror to *Les Demoiselles d'Avignon*, one of the first and most

LEFT: Picasso in 1948, painting an urn in the Madoura ceramic workshops of Georges and Suzanne Ramié, whom he met on a visit to Golfe-Juan in 1946. It was this meeting that inspired Picasso's interest in ceramics.

RIGHT: *The Frugal Repast*, 1904, etching, belongs to Picasso's Blue Period; the theme of blindness appears in many of his works at this time.

famous of his Cubist works, and even Georges Braque at first rejected the painting, although by the end of 1907 he had become one of Picasso's most ardent supporters. For several years the two worked both together and separately to explore to the full the potential of this radically new approach to art.

The collaboration between Braque and Picasso, and with it the most fertile period of Cubism, ended with the outbreak of the First World War, and it is usual to divide the rest of Picasso's life's work, both before and after, into phases – the Blue Period, the Circus Period, the Classical Period. Certainly from the 1920s, however, and arguably from the very outset of his extraordinarily long career, Picasso was working simultaneously in different styles. While certain themes or modes dominated at certain times, all chronological divisions are thus to some extent arbitrary.

John Richardson, author of a magisterial and definitive four-volume biography of the artist, of which the first prize-winning volume was published in 1992 to wide acclaim, initially conceived the project as tracing the artist's development through his portraits of the many women in his life. These images permeated Picasso's style and give some clue to the intensely personal nature of his mysterious and transcendingly creative genius. 'My work is like a diary', he would say to biographers and journalists, and Richardson, a close friend of the artist, was able to observe at first hand how the arrival of a new mistress triggered – or coincided with – a new style.

Another influential factor in Picasso's development right to the end of his life was his Spanish and, in particular, Andalusian heritage. He is now, since publication of his extensive writings, recognized as a major Spanish poet. In his later years in the south of France he delighted in friends who could take him back in spirit to Spain and the informal café circles of likeminded artists and writers that he first enjoyed in Barcelona in his mid-teens and managed to recreate when he moved to Paris. Both Picasso's sense of drama, his ability to adopt new styles and roles without losing his identity, and the blackness of spirit and preoccupation with mortality that becomes increasingly clear in his later work, reflect the artist's Andalusian roots. Similarly, his continuing use of art and sex as metaphors for each other, his fascination with voyeurism and genitalia, is linked with the intensely macho, misogynist and phallocentric nature of Andalusian society.

Pablo Ruiz Picasso was born on October 25, 1881, at Malaga on the southern coast of Spain. He was the first male heir on either side of his family and therefore the cause of much rejoicing, but the birth was a difficult one and apparently the midwife thought he was stillborn and left him while she saw to his mother. Picasso would often tell the story of how his Uncle Salvador, a doctor who smoked large cigars, blew cigar smoke into his infant face, which provoked clear signs of life in the form of a furious cry. Thus the death-in-life theme that was to haunt Picasso's imagination throughout his career was present from the very beginning, together with the element of fable-spinning that was to cause his biographers so much confusion.

His father, José Ruiz Blasco, taught drawing and painting at the provincial school of arts and crafts in Malaga and was also an unoriginal and unsuccessful painter, mainly of pigeons and household pets. The young Picasso was raised in a largely female environment; his maternal grandmother and two aunts lived with his parents and the artist later recalled them as permanent features of his childhood. Some biographers have made much of this female influence, but it was the norm in Andalusian society, where the older men spent most of their free time in the wholly male world of bars and cafés.

During Picasso's childhood the family moved several times to follow father José's teaching career. The first surviving drawings, from the years spent in the Atlantic port of Corunna (where Picasso became a devoted follower of local bullfights) demonstrate that the young Pablo had already mastered academic draftsmanship. Another legend has it that one day in Corunna José asked his son to finish a painting of a pigeon that was giving him trouble, setting the boy to paint the claws. Apparently they were done with such skill that father instantly handed over palette, brushes and paints to son. This story of renunciation would be more convincing if José had in fact given up painting.

In 1895 the family moved to Barcelona, artistic and intellectual capital of Catalonia, which was to provide

the first major stimulus to the fledgling artist. He applied to the local School of Fine Arts, at which his father had taken a teaching post, and was accepted immediately into the more advanced class on the basis of the drawings he submitted. The portraits that he produced during the Corunna years, above all the self-portraits, show him experimenting widely; as he said much later, 'I myself thrash around too much, move too much. You see me here and yet I'm already changed. I'm already elsewhere. I'm never fixed.'

Picasso seems easily to have gained admission to the Madrid art school, the prestigious Royal Academy of San Fernando, in 1897 aged only 16, but the following nine months were unhappy and unproductive. He took an intense dislike to the city and to the traditionalist teaching of the school, fell ill with scarlet fever in the spring of 1898, and went to the mountain village of Horta de Ebro with his friend Manuel Pallares to recuperate. This was the first of several retreats into deep Spanish countryside which were to prove crucial stages in Picasso's development. At Horta he felt himself finally to have escaped from his father's influence, and first began to toy with the idea of dropping his patronym and using only his mother's family name of Picasso.

8

FAR LEFT: *Portrait of Lola*, 1899. Picasso's sister Lola often acted as a model for him during the Barcelona years. This portrait shows Picasso's debt to Impressionists such as Monet, Renoir and Degas, both in subject matter and treatment. At this stage he was still using the name P Ruiz Picasso.

LEFT: The formidable Gertrude Stein who, with her brother Leo, became one of Picasso's first and most influential patrons. She is pictured seated below Picasso's portrait of her.

ABOVE: *Family of Saltimbanques*, 1905. The appearance of circus and harlequin themes in Picasso's work at about this time coincides with a warming of his palette after the rigors of the Blue Period.

Picasso returned to Barcelona in 1899 much more mature and independent than when he had left for Madrid. He refused to re-enrol in the local School of Fine Arts, but instead applied himself to improving his drawing. He also joined a circle of young artists and intellectuals, including art historian Miguel Utrillo, poet Jaime Sabartés and painter Carlos Casagemas. They introduced him to the lively and progressive Catalan school of artists, whose work was related to Symbolism

and Art Nouveau. Sabartés, ironically portrayed as a lily-bearing aesthete in a portrait entitled *A Decadent Poet*, was to become Picasso's devoted friend and served as his secretary and companion for many years from 1935 onward. It was also at this time that Picasso first undertook commercial work to supplement his income, beginning a fruitful line in poster design that was to be pursued spasmodically throughout his career.

It was a natural progression to visit Paris, where

some forty years of avant-garde art could be studied at first hand, and between 1901 and 1904 Picasso alternated his place of residence between Paris and Barcelona. At this stage his stylistic alignments were not fixed, but his social attitudes were much more definite; his sympathy lay with the colorful and dissipated Toulouse-Lautrec, the outsiders Gauguin and Van Gogh, rather than with the more social art of Manet or Renoir. One of his very first Paris paintings portrays the dance hall of the Moulin de la Galette (painted by both Toulouse-Lautrec and Renoir) and stakes his claim to a place in the modern French tradition. Picasso was amazed by the casual Parisian mores, the way couples embraced in the street and were portrayed so doing in contemporary paintings, and his own work became much more explicit as he explored the harnessing of this frank sexuality to his art. He never had a social eye, however; his early paintings of the cafés and night life of Montmartre, sometimes called the Cabaret Period, contain little social observation, few individuals, and do not match the sophistication of his mentors.

During Picasso's second visit to Paris, he met the enterprising young art dealer Ambroise Vollard, who was instrumental in establishing the reputation of many of the Impressionist and Post-Impressionist masters. He agreed to give an exhibition for the young Spaniard, his first in Paris, which was a success, but Vollard lost faith in his protégé when he began to paint in a new, cold style. This was most immediately noticeable in Picasso's choice of colors; the brilliant expressive tones of the Montmartre scenes gave way to a cold, oppressive blue.

This development has been linked with the pain and guilt that Picasso felt over the death of his friend Casagemas, who shot himself in despair over a love affair. Many of the works of the Blue Period are in the form of *memento mori*, evocations of death. Of three paintings of Casagemas on his death bed, only the last truly belongs to the Blue Period and it is also the least anguished, as if with the adoption of a new style Picasso had already exorcized some of his pain. His exploration of the themes of death and decay began in earnest with his return to Barcelona at the beginning of 1902. Blue Period themes are almost invariably desolate; subjects focus on the poor and the outcast – beggars, madmen, the blind, forlorn mothers.

Another canvas of this time, *Child with Dove* (1901)

ABOVE: This *Self-Portrait* of 1907 reflects contemporary interest in native African art.

RIGHT: *The Large Bathers* by Paul Cézanne (1839-1906). Several of the Gosol studies of women reflect Picasso's interest in Cézanne's figure painting, and particularly his great series of *Bather* paintings.

FAR RIGHT: Georges Braque, with whom Picasso developed the first stages of Cubism.

reflects a different facet of this change, however: a mood of empathy and tenderness in sharp contrast to the earlier detached, almost satirical, observation. The compassionate, socially conscious nature of this art has echoes of the work of Millet, the young Van Gogh and Munch late in the previous century, but Picasso's linear virtuosity, evidence of his interest in Spanish Mannerism and above all El Greco, and his monochrome use of color transform these images into something new and intensely personal. One of the most powerful, *The Frugal Meal* (1904), is in fact an etching, one of Picasso's first attempts in this medium, and has been described by one critic as 'a Blue Period masterpiece that paradoxically contains no blue at all'. *La Vie* (1903), which went through many planning stages before reaching the form in which we now know it, is perhaps the most complex and allegorical of these images, and is said to have established Picasso's name and reputation.

In 1904 Picasso again settled in Paris and became the center of an avant-garde circle of writers and artists which included French as well as Spanish members, notably the poet and critic Guillaume Apollinaire. In 1905 he began an affair with Fernande Olivier which was to last six years, his first serious and reasonably durable attachment, and he also acquired his first patrons, the American writer Gertrude Stein and her brother Leo. The more positive tenor that these changes gave to his life was reflected in his work, and above all in his palette; the cold, subdued blues gave way to browns and pinks, and the mood became less austere. *Girl in a Chemise* (c.1905), with its warm coloring, its calm self-confident mood and erotic radiance, contrasts powerfully with the haunted impersonal images that preceded it.

A common enthusiasm in the circle in which Picasso was moving was for the circus and the popular theater, and many of the paintings of the so-called Rose Period show circus and carnival performers, harlequins and dancers, in calm and informal scenes set in a specific context rather than the blue infinity of the earlier work. At the same time, in 1905, Picasso was experimenting with his first sculptural work and it may well be this that led him to study classical sculpture, the influence of which has been discerned in his drawings and watercolors of these months. There is a greater concern with compositional values, volume and balance, and some of his painted nudes began to take on an almost sculptural solidity, foreshadowing the majestic nudes of the 1920s.

In 1906 Picasso and Fernande spent the summer at Gosol in the Urgel valley, a rural, isolated region in the foothills of the Pyrenees, and it was there that he laid the foundations for what was to become Cubism by adopting a new approach to, almost a bypassing of, the classical subjects of art. Before he went to Gosol he was having great difficulty finishing a portrait of Gertrude Stein. He had already begun to reject the kind of traditionalism

that any accepted classical theme necessarily involves, and this process of rejection was inimical to achieving a finished work of art. Much of the work of the Gosol months was tentative, experimental, barely begun, but one image in particular, *The Two Brothers* (1906), attests to the radical path that Picasso was treading. While linked in subject and mood with earlier images of acrobats and circus families, *The Two Brothers* has a luminous, primordial, generic quality that distances it from the accumulated clutter of centuries of art history. On returning to Paris, Picasso found no problem with the Stein portrait; he painted out the face and replaced it with stark, mask-like features partly derived from primitive Iberian sculpture.

Paris in 1907 was in an artistic ferment. The Fauves, dominated by Matisse, were exploring the effects of vivid, non-naturalistic, pure color, a preoccupation which Picasso, who had already demonstrated his relative lack of interest in color as an end in itself, did not share. More significant for the development of Cubism was the general avant-garde interest in primitive African art; some commentators have discerned a 'Negro Period' in Picasso's work at this time. Another crucial stimulus was the major retrospective exhibition of the work of Cézanne, which highlighted that artist's painstaking analysis of nature and his concern with

ABOVE LEFT: *Head of a Woman*, 1909, shows Picasso's interest in sculptural form.

ABOVE RIGHT: Picasso photographed by the surrealist Man Ray.

RIGHT: Picasso's study for the ballet *The Three-Cornered Hat* (1919) was made for Diaghilev's Ballets Russes. His theatrical work fed into the later stages of Cubism.

underlying structure, rather than with the fleeting effects of light that had inspired the Impressionists. In fact, however, Picasso's revolutionary canvas heralding his breakthrough to a new kind of painting, *Les Demoiselles d'Avignon* (1907), was largely completed before the Cézanne exhibition opened. At the time the painting was incomprehensible even to such sympathetic viewers as Matisse and Braque and it was not publicly exhibited until 1937. In structure it harks back to Cézanne's architectural grouping of nude bodies, but in its treatment of form it is as radical a rejection of Impressionism as was the Fauves' use of color. The painting evolved over a considerable period; the central figures have the simplified structure of earlier creations, while the mask-like repose of the heads recalls the portrait of Gertrude Stein. The figures at the side, however, particularly the two on the right, while still constructed of clearly defined planes, are no longer modeled by light but violently hacked out and twisted, in a system of internal torques which is applied to the spatial framework itself as well as to human form and drapery. The traditional norms of classical beauty, the depiction of perceivable reality, the Renaissance rule of the single perspective, are firmly abandoned.

Les Demoiselles d'Avignon proved the point of departure for Cubism. By the autumn of 1908, when the movement was christened by Matisse referring to the *petits cubes* in the work Braque had been doing that

summer, the two painters found that they had separately been tackling the same problem. The concern of Cubism was to create a new method of representing three-dimensional volumes on a two-dimensional surface, which would show objects as they are known and comprehended by the intellect rather than as they appear at a particular time or place. Hence the abandonment of traditional perspective and the adoption of a multiplicity of viewpoints, so that different aspects of the same object can be seen simultaneously.

The movement has traditionally been divided into two phases, the first called 'Analytical' Cubism. While staying again in the small Spanish town of Horta de San Juan in summer 1909, Picasso addressed himself to the problem that he and Braque had posed themselves. He confined his palette to ochers and grays (this move to eliminate color often seems to recur when he was working at the extreme edge of radicalism) and reduced forms and volumes to their simplest geometrical

elements, so creating an all-embracing architectural structure for his vision of the world. A further development came from Picasso's interest in the perfect, faceted form of the crystal, as evidenced, for example in *Man with a Clarinet* (1911-12); his work of 1910-11 becomes both more regularized and more fragmented and ambiguous, achieving an austere yet lyrical discipline that has been compared to Bach's *The Art of the Fugue*.

The problem with abandoning closed form in favor of a planar structure is that the result begins to approach a totally abstract art, which was not the concern of Cubism. Both Picasso and Braque regarded their fragmentation of objects as a means of getting closer to rather than abandoning reality. Synthetic Cubism, the second phase, was both a logical development from the analytical phase and a retreat from abstraction; once the painter has constructed a new world of geometric elements, he can renounce the stationary viewpoint and

reconstitute the object of his painting not on the basis of visual observation but from his idea of it, thus creating a new whole out of fragmentation. Canvases are built up of fewer and bolder flat forms, overlapping and interlocking to produce an effect of almost architectural economy, and colors tend to be somber and elegant.

The new technique of collage played a major role in the development of synthetic Cubism; having destroyed the unity of the object and the unity of space, the inventors of Cubism now sought to destroy the unity of the medium, the painted surface, by introducing 'real' details, as in *Still Life With Chair Caning* (1912) and *Mandolin and Clarinet* (1913). Even when the creative partnership with Braque was at its height, however, Picasso was quite capable of occasionally abandoning all that it stood for and making a wholly 'naturalistic' work, such as the series of drawings of male friends who were not artists which he made in 1915 and which scandalized his avant-garde intimates.

The greater concern with new wholes also led to more interest in decorative effects, evidence of Picasso's simultaneous pursuit of different styles. By the onset of the First World War, which brought to an end the collaboration with Braque, some of Picasso's work was in a vivid, lighthearted vein which has been called 'Rococo' Cubism. This mood was pursued in his work with Diaghilev's Ballets Russes during the war, particularly in his designs for the ballet *Parade*. Picasso's theatrical work in turn fed into Cubism, so that one of the latest manifestations of synthetic Cubism, *The Three Musicians* of 1921, has three figures from the *commedia dell'arte* as its subject and has abandoned the pastel tones of earlier examples for bright primary colors.

Picasso's work for Diaghilev took him to Rome in 1917, in company with Jean Cocteau, and his exposure to antique art, and above all to Roman sculpture, was one factor in the development of a new mood of monumental classicism that characterizes some of his work in the early 1920s. This classical revival was a general European reaction to the chaos of world war, well documented in other arts such as poetry and music – for example, in the work of the avant-garde composer Stravinsky. Picasso's *Two Women Running on the Beach* (1922) and *The Pipes of Pan* (1923), with their solidly sculptural treatment of the human figure, reflect both the general trend and changes in his personal circumstances. In 1918 he had married Olga Koklova, prima ballerina with the Ballets Russes, and in 1921 their son Paul was born; the theme of mother and child plays a part in the more generalized, classically harmonious, almost mythological, atmosphere of his work at this time, the closest Picasso ever came to observing the constraints of bourgeois conformity. And yet at the same time, evidence of his extraordinary virtuosity, Picasso continued also to paint in the synthetic Cubist style, culminating in the monumental series of still lifes in front of open windows which he executed in 1924.

Picasso never stood still; *The Three Dancers* of 1925 is a decisive rejection, both in scale (the figures are nearly lifesize, reminiscent of the scale of Picasso's drop curtain design for *Parade*) and in mood, of many of the subjects that had preoccupied him in recent years. The grace of the ballet and the calm poise of the classical women and youths are replaced by galvanized, emaciated figures conveying a sense of obsessive movement and violence. The influence of Surrealism has been suggested to explain the disquieting, convulsive features of this work, and Picasso was certainly closely in touch with André Breton, the movement's founder, at this time. He himself always disclaimed any connection with Surrealism, however, and his work as a whole is too deeply concerned with the analysis of forms, with the conceptual rather than the purely visual, to be compatible with the irrationalist subconscious elements of Surrealism.

The implications of *The Three Dancers* for Picasso's subsequent work were immense. The violently expressive mood, the distorted human figures, the bitterness and anguish, all recur in a series of works in the late 1920s and 1930s and culminate in his most famous painting of all, *Guernica* (1937). The series of distorted human images that he produced at this time, as far as one can tell wholly female and always confined within an enclosed structural space, is among his best known and also most controversial work. In *The Painter and His Model* (1926), the laterally extended format allows a less tortured, more fluid overall line, although the detailing remains frenzied.

The sheer range of Picasso's sources and the diversity of styles on which he could draw are perhaps most clearly illustrated in the tiny *Crucifixion* (1930), which is usually taken to be a halfway point between *The Three Dancers* and *Guernica*: this contains Christian, pagan and classical references, motifs from Minoan and Australian aboriginal art, all in dissonant, primary colors. Concurrent with the disturbing savagery of this image, however, Picasso was working on a number of paintings, such as *Large Still Life with Pedestal Table* (1931), which reflect a very different, both calmer and more decorative, mood; it has been suggested that these were inspired by his new mistress, Marie-Thérèse Walter. Another theme that he explored in the early 1930s and

LEFT: This plate from 1957 shows Picasso's mastery of ceramic techniques.

ABOVE: Picasso (second from right) in Antibes in 1937, with current mistress Dora Maar (right) and photographer Man Ray (front). Picasso moved permanently to the French Mediterranean coast in 1946.

RIGHT: Picasso as sculptor; this bronze *Goat* (1950) was created from a plaster cast formed round a wicker basket for the stomach, cast iron legs and two clay pots for the udders.

LEFT: *Bust of Sylvette*, now in University Plaza, New York City. Picasso's interest in monumental sculpture dates from the rediscovery of early Iberian work in the first decade of the twentieth century but received an impetus in the 1950s, when the Norwegian Carl Nestar taught him the technique of carving concrete.

BELOW: Picasso as grand old man, in his studio with the young Brigitte Bardot.

BELOW: *Peace*, 1962, Picasso's poster for the World Congress for Disarmament and Peace.

which reappeared in *Guernica* was the mythological image of the Minotaur, extended after a long visit to Spain in 1934 to include the bullfight.

The outbreak of civil war in Spain in 1936 found Picasso firmly in the Republican camp, and his first work dealing with the theme was a series of etchings called *The Dream and Lie of Franco*, made early in 1937. He was then commissioned to paint a large canvas for the Spanish Republic's pavilion at the World Fair in Paris, due to open in summer 1937. He had not yet begun work on this when news broke of the bombing on April 28 of the Basque town of Guernica by German planes in the service of Franco; by May 1 he was making his first sketches. The result has been described by one critic as 'the high point of his mythological creations, and . . . one of the masterpieces of twentieth-century painting, its most distilled, most passionate expression.' In the final version Picasso's mythical figures are linked within a triangular form that recalls the pediment of a Greek temple. Inside it all is despair and confusion – the dying horse, the desperate woman in a burning house, the warrior with the broken sword, the mourning woman at left holding her child. Several of these images, particularly *The Weeping Woman*, reappear in similarly apocalyptic works of the period, but in this case in

strikingly dissonant colors, in contrast to the austere palette of black, white and gray which helps to reinforce the paralyzing terror of *Guernica*.

Picasso spent the years of the Second World War closeted in his Paris studio, emerging with the liberation a universally acclaimed master; a large hall was reserved for his works alone at the Salon de Libération held in Paris in fall 1944. A move to the Mediterranean coast in 1946 introduced a more idyllic spirit, a world of fauns and centaurs, into his previously anguished mythological representations. As his private life again took a happier turn, his paintings reflected this more settled atmosphere (*The Studio at La Californie*, 1956). He also undertook a series of dialogues with old masters, including fifteen variations on Delacroix's *Femmes d'Alger* and forty-four on Velasquez's *Las Meninas* (1957). This later output does not compare in sheer momentousness with the pre-war years, and Picasso showed little awareness of the next major postwar wave of painting. By the 1960s he was concentrating largely on graphic work, and some commentators have dismissed altogether the painting of his last two decades. Certainly there was nothing new, and yet canvases such as *The Kiss* (1969) demonstrate the continuing ability, extraordinary in a almost ninety-year-old man, to create a vital and arresting image.

LEFT
Portrait of the Artist's Mother
1896, pastel on paper
Picasso Museum, Barcelona

ABOVE
Salon del Prado
1897, oil on wood, 25⅜×6½ inches (10×15.5cm)
Picasso Museum, Barcelona

ABOVE
In the Dressing Room
1900, pastel on paper, 18⅞×20⅞ inches (48×53cm)
Picasso Museum, Barcelona

OVERLEAF LEFT
The Embrace in the Street
1900, pastel on paper, 22¼×13¾ inches (59×35cm)
Picasso Museum, Barcelona

LEFT
Sabartés as a Decadent Poet
1900, oil and watercolor on paper, 18⅞×12½ inches (48×32cm)
Picasso Museum, Barcelona

OVERLEAF RIGHT
Self-Portrait
1901, oil on canvas, 31×23⅝ inches (79×60cm)
Picasso Museum, Paris

23

LEFT
Child with a Dove
1901, oil on canvas, 28³/₈×21¹/₄ inches (73×45cm)
Anonymous loan to the National Gallery, London

ABOVE
The Blind Man's Meal
1903, oil on canvas, 37¹/₂×37¹/₂ inches (95.3×94.6cm)
Metropolitan Museum of Art, NY, Gift of Mr and Mrs Ira
Haupt

The Death of Casegemas
1901, oil on wood,
10⅝×13⅞ inches (27×35cm)
Picasso Museum, Paris

The Tragedy
1903, oil on wood, 41½×27⅛ inches (105.4×69cm)
National Gallery of Art, Washington, Chester Dale Collection

La Vie
1903, oil on canvas, 77½×50⅛ inches (197×127.3cm)
The Cleveland Museum of Art, Gift of the Hanna Fund, 45.24

LEFT
The Actor
1905, oil on canvas, 76³/8×44¹/8 inches (194×112cm)
Metropolitan Museum of Art, NY

ABOVE
Circus Artist and Child
1905, watercolor drawing on paper, 6⅞×4¹/8 inches
(16.8×10.5cm)
Tate Gallery, London

31

Saltimbanques
1905, oil on canvas, 82¾×90½ inches (212.8×229.6cm)
National Gallery of Art, Washington, Chester Dale Collection

Girl in a Chemise
c.1905, oil on canvas, 28⅝×23⅝ inches (72.7×60cm)
Tate Gallery, London

Spanish Woman from the Island of Majorca
(sketch for painting 'Les Bateleurs')
1905, gouache on cardboard, 29½×20 inches
(75×51cm)
Pushkin Fine Arts Museum, Moscow

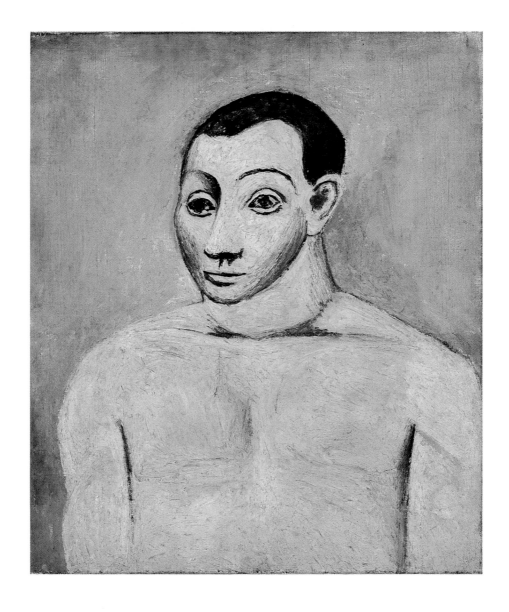

LEFT
The Two Brothers
1906, gouache on cardboard, 31½×23¼ inches
(80×59cm)
Picasso Museum, Paris

ABOVE
Self-portrait
1906, oil on canvas, 36¼×28¾ inches (92×73cm)
Picasso Museum, Paris

Gertrude Stein
1906, oil on canvas, 39¼×32 inches (99.7×81.3cm)
Metropolitan Museum of Art, NY, Bequest of Gertrude Stein
1946

The Toilette
1906, oil on canvas, 59½×39 inches (151×99cm)
Allbright-Knox Art Gallery, Buffalo, NY, Fellows for Life of
1926 Fund

ABOVE
Reclining Nude
1906, gouache on paper, 18⅝×24⅛ inches
(47.3×61.3cm)
The Cleveland Museum of Art, Gift of Mr and Mrs Michael
Straight, 54.865

RIGHT
Negro Dancer
1907, oil on canvas, 24⅞×16¾ inches (63×42.5cm)
Thyssen-Bornemisza Collection, Lugano

Seated Nude (Study for 'Les Demoiselles d'Avignon')
1906-7, oil on canvas, 47⅝×36⅞ inches (121×93.5cm)
Picasso Museum, Paris

Les Demoiselles d'Avignon
1907 oil on canvas, 96×92 inches (243.8×233.7cm)
The Museum of Modern Art, New York, acquired through the
Lillie P Bliss Bequest

LEFT
Nude Figure
1910, oil on canvas, 38½×30 inches
(97.8×76.2cm)
Albright-Knox Art Gallery, Buffalo, New
York, Consolidated Purchase Funds, 1954

RIGHT
Man with a Mandolin
1911, oil on canvas, 63⅞×28 inches
(162×71cm)
Picasso Museum, Paris

LEFT
Man with a Clarinet
1911-12, oil on canvas, 41¼×27⅛ inches (105×69cm)
Thyssen-Bornemisza Collection, Lugano

BELOW
Violin and Sheet of Music
*1912, pasted colored papers and musical score on
cardboard, gouache, 30¾×25 inches (78×63.5cm)*
Picasso Museum, Paris

Still Life with Chair Caning
1912, oil and oilcloth on canvas edged with rope, 29×37 inches (73.7×94cm)
Picasso Museum, Paris

Mandolin and Clarinet
1913, construction: fir components with paint and crayon strokes, 22⅞×14¼×9⅛ inches (58×36×23cm)
Picasso Museum, Paris

ABOVE
Glass, Pipe, Ace of Clubs and Die
1914, painted wooden and metal components on wooden base painted in oils, 13³⁄₈×3¼ inches (34×8.5cm)
Picasso Museum, Paris

RIGHT
Man with a Pipe
1914, oil on printed textile pasted on canvas, 54¼×26¼ inches (138×66.5cm)
Picasso Museum, Paris

BELOW
Restaurant Still Life
1914, oil and sawdust on cardboard, 11⅝×15 inches
(29.5×38cm)
Hermitage Museum, St Petersburg

RIGHT
Harlequin
1915, oil on canvas, 72¼×41⅜ inches (183.5×105.2cm)
The Museum of Modern Art, New York, acquired through the
Lillie P Bliss Bequest

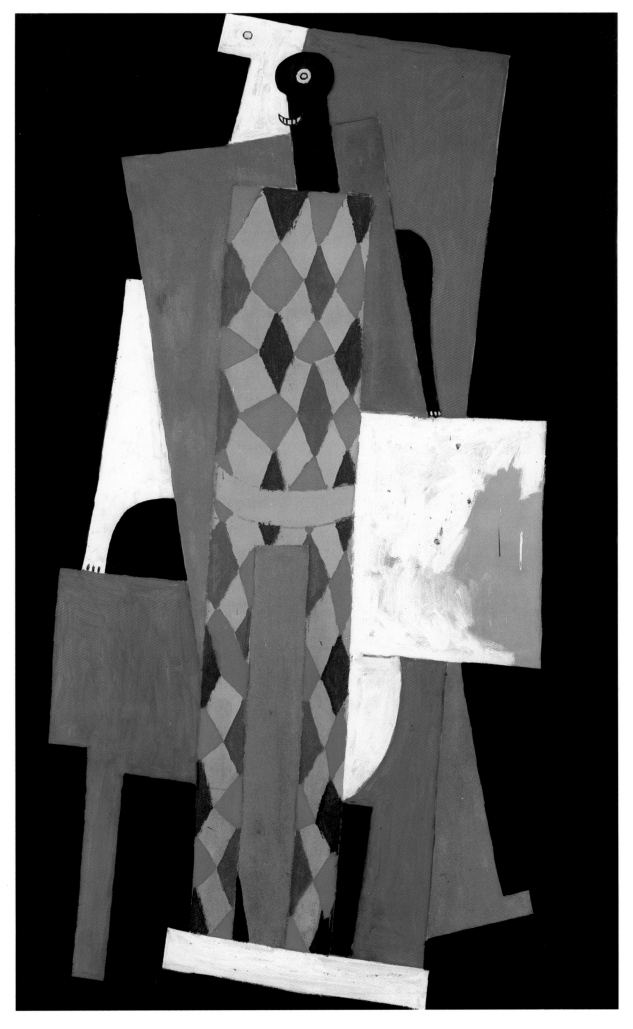

RIGHT
Still Life with Grapes and Pear
1914, oil on board
Private collection

LEFT
Glass, Bouquet, Guitar and Bottle
1919, oil on canvas
Private collection, Paris

ABOVE
The Three Musicians
1921, oil on canvas, 79×87¾ inches (200.7×222.9cm)
The Museum of Modern Art, New York, Mrs Simon
Guggenheim Fund

ABOVE
Manola with Pointillist Technique
1917, oil on canvas, 46½×35 inches (118×89 cm)
Picasso Museum, Barcelona

RIGHT
Portrait of Olga in an Armchair
1917, oil on canvas, 51¼×35 inches (130×88.8cm)
Picasso Museum, Paris

Seated Pierrot
1918, oil on canvas, 36¾×29¼ inches (93.3×74.3cm)
The Museum of Modern Art, New York

The Bathers
1918, oil on canvas, 10⅝×8¾ inches (27×22cm)
Picasso Museum, Paris

Still Life with Pitcher and Apples
1919, oil on canvas, 25⅝×17 inches (65×43cm)
Picasso Museum, Paris

Three Women at the Fountain
1921, sanguine on canvas, 78¾×63⅜ inches
(200×161cm)
Picasso Museum, Paris

Two Women Running on a Beach (The Race)
1922, gouache on plywood, 12⅞×16¼ inches
(32.5×41.1cm)
Picasso Museum, Paris

Saltimbanque with Crossed Arms
1923, oil on canvas
Private collection

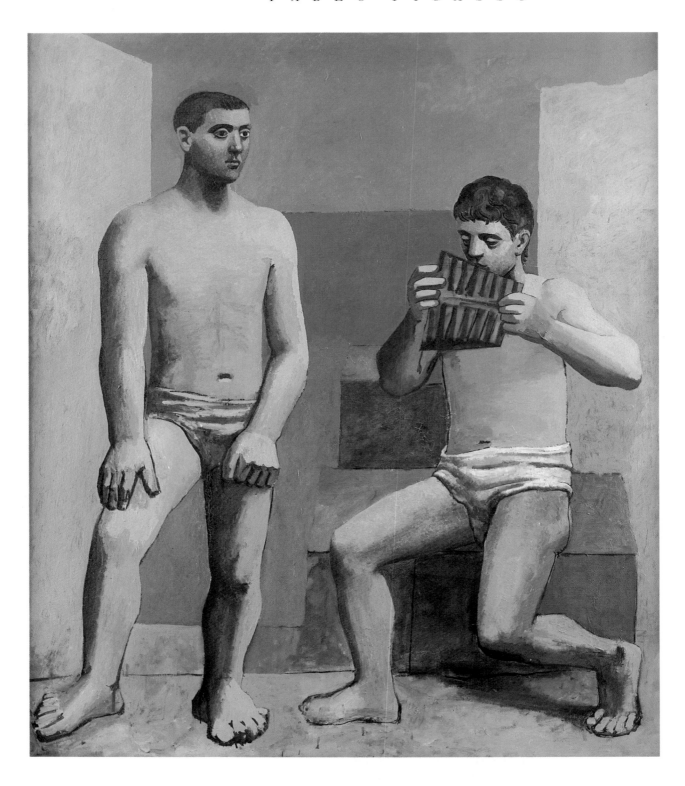

ABOVE
The Pipes of Pan
1923, oil on canvas, 80¾×68½ inches (205×174cm)
Picasso Museum, Paris

RIGHT
Harlequin with a Mirror
1923, oil on canvas, 39½×32 inches (100.3×81.3cm)
Thyssen-Bornemisza Collection, Lugano, Switzerland

OVERLEAF LEFT
Paul as Harlequin
1924, oil on canvas, 52×38¾ inches (132×98.4cm)
Picasso Museum, Paris

OVERLEAF RIGHT
Paul as Pierrot
1925, oil on canvas, 51¼×38¼ (130×97cm)
Picasso Museum, Paris

PABLO PICASSO

LEFT
The Three Dancers
1925, oil on canvas, 84¾×56 inches (215.3×142.2cm)
Tate Gallery, London

BELOW
Figure and Profile
1928, oil on canvas, 28¼×25⅝ inches (72×60cm)
Picasso Museum, Paris

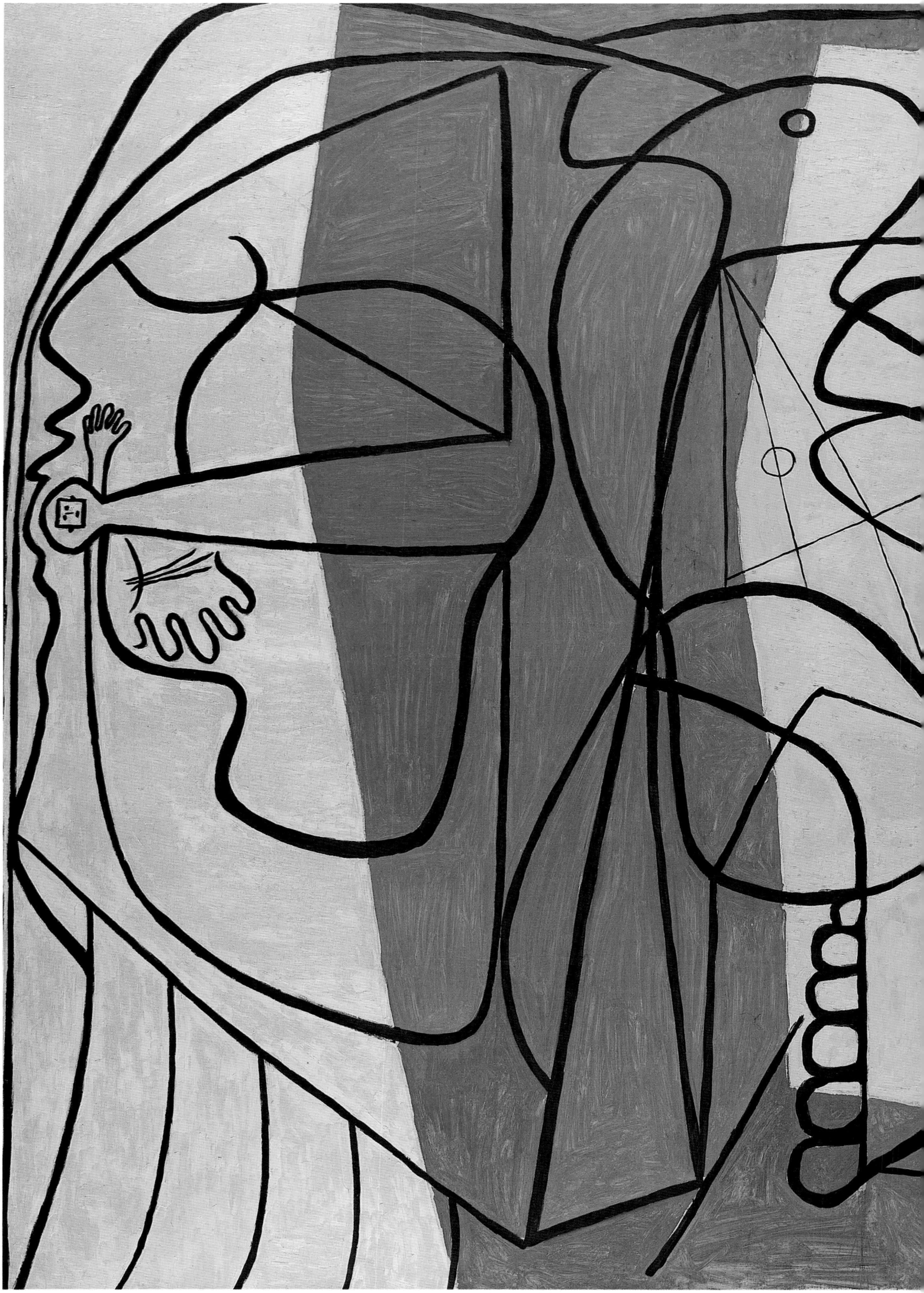

PREVIOUS PAGES
The Painter and his Model
1926, oil on canvas, 67³/₄×100⁷/₈ inches (172×256cm)
Picasso Museum, Paris

ABOVE
Head of a Woman
1929, oil on canvas
Private collection

RIGHT
Large Still Life with Pedestal Table
1931, oil on canvas, 76⁷/₈×51³/₈ inches (195×130.5cm)
Picasso Museum, Paris

RIGHT
The Crucifixion
1930, oil on plywood, 20¼×26¼
inches (51.5×66.5cm)
Picasso Museum, Paris

OVERLEAF
Figures on the Seashore
1931, oil on canvas, 51¼×76⅞
inches (130×195cm)
Picasso Museum, Paris

ABOVE
Reclining Nude
1932, oil on canvas, 51¼×63¾ inches (130×166.7cm)
Picasso Museum, Paris

RIGHT
Woman in a Red Armchair
1932, oil on canvas, 51¼×38¼ inches (130.2×97cm)
Picasso Museum, Paris

LEFT
Girl before a Mirror
1932, oil on canvas, 64×51¼ inches (162.6×130.2cm)
The Museum of Modern Art, New York, Gift of Mrs Simon
Guggenheim

ABOVE
Composition with a Butterfly
*1932, cloth, wood, plants, string, drawing pin, butterfly
and oil paint on canvas, 6¼×8⅝×1 inch
(16×22×2.5cm)*
Picasso Museum, Paris

Bullfight: Death of the Woman Toreador
1933, oil and crayon on wood panel,
8½×10⅝ inches (21.7×27cm)
Picasso Museum, Paris

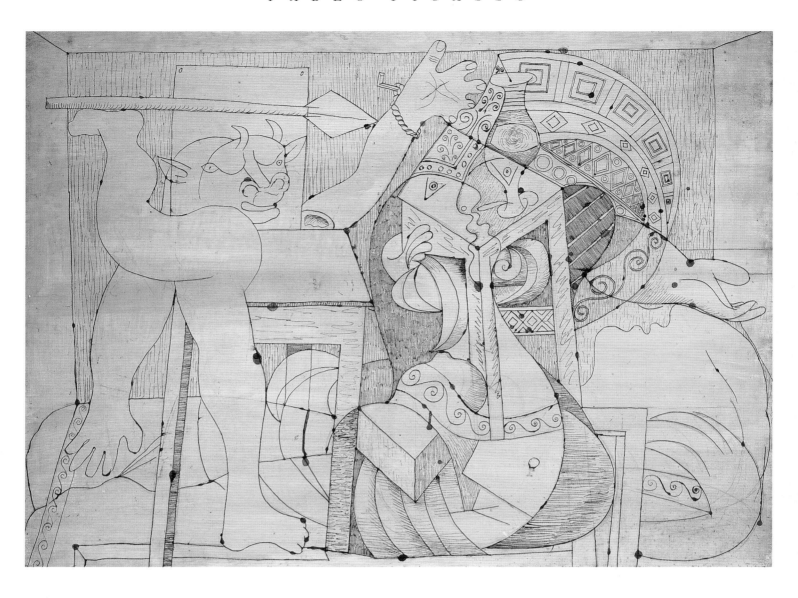

ABOVE
Minotaur with a Javelin
1934, india ink on plywood, 38¼×51¼ inches
(97×130cm)
Picasso Museum, Paris

RIGHT
Portrait of Marie-Thérèse
1937, oil on canvas, 25⅜×31⅞ inches (100×81cm)
Picasso Museum, Paris

Sleeping Woman with Shutters
1936, oil and charcoal on canvas, 21½×26¾ inches (54.5×65.2cm)
Picasso Museum, Paris

RIGHT
Portrait of Dora Maar
1936, oil on canvas, 25½×21¼ inches (65×54cm)
Private collection, Paris

LEFT
Portrait of Dora Maar
1937, oil on canvas, 36¼×25⅝ inches (92×65cm)
Picasso Museum, Paris

BELOW
Weeping Woman
1937, oil on canvas, 23½×38¼ inches (59.7×48.9cm)
Tate Gallery, London

ABOVE
Dish of Pears
1936, oil on canvas, 15×24 inches (38.1×61cm)
Tate Gallery, London

RIGHT
Maya with her Doll
1938, oil on canvas, 28⅞×23⅝ inches (73.5×60cm)
Picasso Museum, Paris

Guernica
1937, oil on canvas, 138×308 inches (350×782.3cm)
Prado, Madrid

BALLETS RUSSES
DE DIAGHILEW
1909 - 1929

MARS - AVRIL 1939

MUSÉE DES ARTS DÉCORATIFS
Palais du Louvre _ Pavillon de Marsan, 107, rue de Rivoli

ENTRÉE 6 FRANCS

LEFT
Ballets Russes de Diaghilev
Exhibition poster for Ballets Russes
1939, Lithograph, 23⅝×15¾ inches (60×40cm)
Private collection

ABOVE
Woman in Green
1943, oil on canvas, 51×38 inches (129.5×96.5cm)
Collection of Ciannait Sweeney, New York

PABLO PICASSO

Cat Catching a Bird
1939, oil on canvas, 31⁷/₈×39³/₈ inches
(81×100cm)
Picasso Museum, Paris

RIGHT
Café at Royan
*1940, oil on canvas,
38¼×15¼ inches
(97.2×38.7cm)*
Picasso Museum, Paris

OVERLEAF
Vert-Galant Square
*1943, oil on canvas, 25⅜×36¼
inches (64.5×92cm)*
Picasso Museum, Paris

LEFT
First Steps
1943, oil on canvas, 51¼×38¼ inches (130.2×97.2cm)
Yale University Art Gallery, Gift of Stephen C Clark BA 1903

ABOVE
The Charnel House
1944-45, oil and charcoal on canvas, 78⅝×98½ inches (200×250.1cm)
The Museum of Modern Art, New York, acquired through the
Mrs Sam A Lewisohn Bequest (by exchange) and Mrs Bernard
in memory of her husband Dr Bernard, William Rubin, and
Anonymous Funds.

ABOVE
Head of a Faun
1947, gouache
Private collection

ABOVE
Blue Owl
1947, oil on canvas, 48¾×40¼ inches (123×102cm)
Private collection

Goat's Skull, Bottle and Candle
1952, oil on canvas, 35⅛×45¾ inches
(89.2×116.2cm)
Tate Gallery, London

Two Children (Claude Drawing with Paloma)
1952, oil on canvas, 36¼×28¾ inches (92.1×73cm)
Private collection (Art Resource/Scala)

Bulls in Vallauris
1955, linocut poster, 35×23⅜ inches (88.9×59.4cm)

The Metropolitan Museum of Art, New York, The Mr and Mrs
Charles Kramer Collection, gift of Mr and Mrs Charles Kramer
1979

ABOVE
Women of Algiers (after Delacroix),
1955, oil on canvas, 44⅞×57½ inches (113.8×146.1cm)
Collection of Mr and Mrs Victor W Ganz, New York

RIGHT
The Infanta Margarita
1957, oil on canvas, 39⅜×32 inches (100×81cm)
Picasso Museum, Barcelona

ABOVE
Spring
1956, oil on canvas, 51×76½ inches (129.5×194.3cm)
Private collection, Paris (Art Resource)

RIGHT
Vallauris Exhibition
1956, linocut poster, 39⅜×25⅞ inches (100×65.7cm)
The Metropolitan Museum of Art, New York, the Mr and Mrs
Charles Kramer collection, gift of Mr and Mrs Charles Kramer,
1979

OVERLEAF LEFT
Las Meninas (The Doves 1)
1957, oil on canvas, 31½×39⅜ inches (80×100cm)
Picasso Museum, Barcelona

OVERLEAF RIGHT
Picasso: Ceramics and White Pottery Exhibition
1958, linocut poster, 26×19⅜ inches (66×49.2cm)
The Metropolitan Museum of Art, New York, the Mr and Mrs
Charles Kramer collection, gift of Mr and Mrs Charles Kramer,
1979

RIGHT
Women and Goats
1959, color linocut, 20⅞×25¼ inches (53×64cm)
Private collection

OVERLEAF
Le Déjeuner sur l'Herbe (after Manet)
1960, oil on canvas, 51¼×76⅞ inches (130×195cm)
Picasso Museum, Paris

OVERLEAF, PAGES 122/123
Painter and Model
1963, oil on canvas, 51¼×76⅞ inches (130×195cm)
Private collection

The Kiss
1969, oil on canvas,
38¼×51¼ inches (97×130cm)
Picasso Museum, Paris

15.7.70.

ABOVE
Painter and Model
1970, colored crayon and chalk on cardboard, 8½×11⅛ inches (21.8×28.2cm)
Private collection

RIGHT
The Matador
1970, oil on canvas, 57¼×44⅞ inches (145.5×114cm)
Picasso Museum, Paris

Acknowledgments

The publisher would like to thank Mike and Sue Rose, Casebourne Rose, Brighton, who designed this book, and the following agencies and institutions for supplying illustrative material.

Allbright-Knox Art Gallery, Buffalo, New York: pages 39, 44

Art Resource: pages 7, 9 (top), 46, 67, 74, 114

Art Resource/Bridgeman Art Library: page 41

Art Resource/Giraudon: pages 12 (left), 56, 60, 65, 89, 126

Art Resource/Scala: pages 16 (top), 97, 110, 112

Bettmann Archive: pages 6, 9 (below), 11, 12 (right), 15 (top), 16 (below), 106, 107

Cleveland Museum of Art: 29, 40

ET Archive: pages 54-55, 122-123

Gallery of the Twentieth Century, Berlin: page 10 (left)

Hermitage Museum, St Petersburg/ET Archive: page 53

Metropolitan Museum of Modern Art, New York: pages 25, 30, 39, 111, 115, 117

The Museum of Modern Art, New York: pages 13 (Collection

Paul Rosenberg), 43, 53, 57, 82, 105

Museum of Modern Art, Moscow/Bridgeman Art Library: page 2

National Gallery, London: page 24 (anonymous loan)

National Gallery of Art, Washington: pages 28, 32-33

Petit Palais, Paris: page 10 (right)

Picasso Museum, Barcelona: pages 8, 18, 19, 20, 21, 22, 58, 113, 116

Picasso Museum, Paris: pages 1, 3, 9 (right), 14, 15 (below), 23, 26-27, 36, 37, 42, 45, 47, 48, 49, 50, 51, 59, 61, 62, 63, 64, 66, 68, 69, 71, 72/73, 75, 76-77, 78-79, 80, 81, 83, 84-85, 86, 87, 88, 90, 93, 98-99, 100-101, 102-103, 120-121, 124-125, 127

Prado, Madrid: page 94-95

Private Collection: pages 17, 96, 118-119

Pushkin Fine Arts Museum, Moscow/Novosti Press Agency: page 35

Tate Gallery, London: pages 31, 34, 70, 91, 92, 108-109

Yale University Art Gallery: page 104